A Dog's Life

A Play in One Act

Pam Valentine

A Samuel French Acting Edition

FOUNDED 1830

SAMUELFRENCH.COM
SAMUELFRENCH-LONDON.CO.UK

FOR PRODUCTION ENQUIRIES

UNITED STATES AND CANADA
Info@SamuelFrench.com
1-866-598-8449

UNITED KINGDOM AND EUROPE
Theatre@SamuelFrench-London.co.uk
020-7255-4302

Each title is subject to availability from Samuel French, depending upon country of performance. Please be aware that *A DOG'S LIFE* may not be licensed by Samuel French in your territory. Professional and amateur producers should contact the nearest Samuel French office or licensing partner to verify availability.

CHARACTERS

The Dogs

Ben, a battered old mongrel. Male
Fritz, a German Shepherd. Tough and rough. Male
Fifi, an overweight poodle. Female
Ginger, a bouncy and excitable young pup. Male or female

The Humans

The **Warden**
The **Woman** Visitor

The play is set in an animal shelter
Time —The present

AUTHOR'S NOTE

Costumes

The costumes suggest the lives of the dogs. There is no attempt
to portray them as animals. Ben has a scarf round his neck, old
trousers tied with string and a collarless shirt or T- shirt. Fritz
wears an army combat shirt and trousers. Fifi has a black
leotard with frills on the wrists and ankles. Ginger, who can be
played by either sex, wears a suitably coloured leotard. None
of the dogs wears shoes and they either sit or remain on all
fours throughout.

Pam Valentine

Dedicated to my dog
Woof

Also by Pam Valentine,
published by Samuel French Ltd

Day of Reckoning

A DOG'S LIFE

An animal shelter

This play can be most effectively set against a black backdrop or curtains. A metal structure suggests four cages, each of which has a blanket bed in the corner. In the cages, from L to R, are Fifi, Fritz, Ben and Ginger. Ben is asleep; Ginger is chewing a rubber toy

There is a sudden noise of loud barking, off. Fifi looks pained. Fritz is instantly alert. Ben opens one eye, sighs, then closes his eye. Ginger tosses whatever he is chewing into the air

Fifi (*who has a faint French accent*) Oh ... This noise — I simply cannot stand it!

Ben Every time I drop off ...

Ginger What is it? What's happening? Is it food? Is it? Is it?

Fritz (*irritably*) Food is at five. You should know that by now. (*He puts his head on one side and listens*) I think it is the quarantine block ... Yes. It is.

Ginger Quarantine? What's quarantine? Is it food? Is it? Is it?

Fritz Sh! (*He listens*) Ah! A new arrival. He thinks he is there for ever. Must be his first time. (*He listens again*) Ah — they are telling him ...

The barking slowly fades to silence

Ginger Ben! Ben! What's quarantine?

Ben (*after a yawn*) Quarantine is where they put you when you've been abroad, Ginger.

Ginger Abroad? What's abroad? Is it food? Is it? Is it?

Fritz I am going to kill that pup.

Ginger Tell me! What's abroad?

Ben (*who doesn't know*) Well now, it's — er — it's sort of ... It's ... It's ... Fritz?

Fritz Abroad. (*He thinks*) Abroad is — there. It is not here. So it must be there.

Fifi Typical German logic.

Fritz What would an overweight French hearthrug know about logic?

Fifi How dare you! I have won prizes.

Ben Not again ...

Fritz Prizes? With that fat belly?

Fritz and Fifi snarl at each other

Ben Stop it! The pair of you. Fine example you both are for a young pup with his life in front of him. If he picks up aggressive tendencies from you two he's never going to get himself adopted.

Ginger What's adopted? Is it food? Is it? Is it?

Fritz He should be in the puppy block. He should not be here with us.

Ben They're full to bursting in the puppy block. When Brown Coat took me to see White Coat I heard them talking. Every August it's the same, they said. Then it's like it again in January.

Fritz I know about this August. Humans call it the "Holiday Season." They put their pups into kennels and do not take them out. I have heard them: "See you in a fortnight," they say. And that is that.

Fifi This is because they chew. Humans do not like chewy puppies.

Ginger Am I a chewy puppy? Am I? Am I?

Ben Well, now let's think. You had a rubber bone this morning ... Where is it now?

Ginger (*going from place to place*) There's — one bit here and — another bit here and — another bit ... (*He snuffles all round his cage*)

Fifi My humans always took me on holiday with them. First, I went to the beauty parlour. I was shampooed and clipped and made to look truly exquisite ...

Fritz Typically stupid human behaviour.
Fifi We went to the best hotels. And everyone used to say "Oh, look
at Fifi! Isn't she sweet?" I was adored ...
Fritz Adored.
Fifi Yes! Adored.
Fritz Then why are you here? If you were so adored?

Fifi looks at him then sinks into a disconsolate heap

Ben That's quite enough of that. No need to upset her. No need at
all.
Ginger Shall I tell you why I'm here, Fritz? Shall I? Shall I?
Fritz No.
Ginger I'm here because ——
Fritz I said 'No'.

Ginger snuffles around his cage again

Ben (*to Fritz*) You're all heart, you are. (*To Ginger*) All right then,
young pup, why are you here? I said — why are you here?

Ginger snuffles more frantically

Hey! I'm talking to you!
Ginger Biscuit. I can smell biscuit. Biscuit! Biscuit! Biscuit! (*He
follows the scent into a corner, pulls a blanket from his bed and
finds a piece of biscuit*)

Ben watches Ginger with affectionate amusement

Ben They're always hungry at that age.
Fifi I have been hungry since I arrived. Still, I must think positively.
By the time I am adopted I will be down to my target weight.

Fritz shakes with laughter

What is so funny?
Fritz By the time anyone adopts you you will have disappeared
altogether.

Fifi (*hysterically*) I will be adopted. I will. I am still young. And
once I have been to the beauty parlour ——

*Fritz rolls on his back with laughter. Fifi looks at him. She has an
idea, narrows her eyes, straightens her shoulders and sings "La
Marseillaise." Fritz is outraged. He springs to his feet and loudly
sings "Deutchland Uber Alles". The noise is deafening*

Ben They'll be the death of me, those two.
Ginger What are they doing?
Ben Trying to kill me, that's what they're doing. Shut up, both of
you.

*Fritz and Fifi sing loudly. Ginger runs round and round in circles
shouting "Shut up"*

  The Warden enters L. *He wears a brown overall*

Warden What the hell's going on in here? It's worse than the
quarantine block. That's enough. Quiet! (*Very loudly*) Quiet!

Slowly the dogs subside. Only Ginger still circles madly

  (*Moving to Ginger's cage*) OK, calm down, calm down. Teaching
him bad ways, you lot are. Come on! Good boy! (*He takes a
chocolate button from his pocket and offers it to Ginger*)

Ginger bounces up and tries to take the button

Warden Hey! Just a minute. What did I teach you yesterday?
Fritz Oh no ... Not the sit routine ...
Warden Sit!

Ginger looks at the Warden, puzzled

Fritz Why? Why do they do this?
Warden Sit!

Ben Makes 'em feel powerful.
Warden I said "Sit"!
Ben (*quietly*) Sit down, Ginger, there's a good pup.

Ginger sits

Warden Good boy! Very good. And the paw? What do we do with
our paw?

*Behind the Warden's back, Ben, Fritz, and Fifi, with bored
expressions, all hold up a paw. Ginger puts his head on one side and
looks at the Warden*

Come on! Where's that paw? Like this! Remember? (*He holds
one hand up like a paw*)

The other dogs shake with laughter

Fritz Have they no idea how stupid they look?
Warden Don't you want a little treat?
Ginger Is it food? Is it? Is it?
Warden It's no good you squeaking at me. Where's your paw?
Ben Ginge!

Ginger looks at Ben. Ben holds up a paw. Ginger copies him

Warden Well done. You see? You can do it.

The Warden gives Ginger a chocolate button. Ginger is ecstatic

Fritz All that for one doggie choc. What do they think we are ... ?
Ben Whatever they want us to be ... ?

The Warden goes to Ben's cage

Warden Hallo, Ben, old boy! Too tired to move, are we? (*He looks
at Ben and thinks for a moment*) How long have you been with us
now ... ? (*He takes a notebook from his pocket*)

Fritz As if he could understand the answer ...
Warden (*looking in his notebook*) A lot longer than you should
have been ... (*He looks sadly at Ben, then moves on to Fritz*) And
how are you, Fritz? You feeling any friendlier today?

Fritz growls

Please yourself. (*He moves on to Fifi who holds up a paw*)
Warden Nice try, Fifi, but I don't think so. In fact ... (*He looks at
her*) I think we'll cut down on your biscuit for a few days. (*He
writes in the notebook*)
Fifi (*outraged*) Cut down my ... Is he mad? All I need is a good trim.
Fritz And ten miles round the park every day.

Fifi moves to the bars that separate her from Fritz

Fifi If I ever get my teeth through these bars ...
Fritz What? What will you do?

Fifi and Fritz snarl at each other

Ben Don't fight in front of a human - looks bad . . .
Warden Now then! Behave yourselves.   You've got a visitor
coming round in a minute.
Fifi Visitor? At this time?
Ginger Visitor? What's a visitor? Is it food? Is it? Is it?
Warden Play your cards right, look appealing, don't jump up,
and one of you could be on the way to a new home.

*The Warden puts his notebook back in his pocket, walks back past
the cages, pausing to look at Ben, and exits*

Ben watches the Warden go, wondering

Fifi (*longingly*) Titbits ...
Fritz (*fiercely*) Something to guard!

Ginger What's happening? What's happening? Ben, tell me, what's happening?

Ben What? Oh, there's a human coming. A human who wants a dog. Going to give us all the once-over. And — if one of us takes their fancy ——

Ginger Me! Me! Then I can see my brothers and sisters again.

The other three look at each other

Fritz Someone had better tell him.

Ben Ginger, once you come here — that's it. Sorry — but ...

Ginger What? What?

Ben You don't see your brothers and sisters again. Not once you come here. Well, not generally — I've never known it happen; have you, Fritz?

Fritz Never.

Ginger Never? Never ever?

Ben shakes his head

Why not?

Ben Because what happens is, with pups, you only stay together for a while. Then ... you go your ways. You don't stay together. That's not how humans do it.

Ginger We went in the big bag together.

Fifi What big bag?

Ginger We couldn't breathe. We tried to get out but we couldn't. We just couldn't. It was wet — and cold — and we cried.

Fifi It must have been a sack ...

Ben Thrown in a river ...

Fritz Barbaric.

Ben Oh — they do much worse things to each other. I've seen them fight. Knives — bricks — bottles ...

Fritz (*puzzled*) I wonder why they don't use their teeth ...

Ben Too simple, I suppose. (*To Ginger*) Lucky for you someone fished you out, young Ginger!

Fifi Was it? (*She looks round*) Look at us ... Perhaps we'd all be better off at the bottom of the river.

Ben Now then. Never say die till you're dead, Fifi.

Fifi I think I would rather be dead. When you have been loved — truly loved ...

Ben (*with absolute certainty*) You've been lucky.

Fritz I wonder who gave them the power ...

Ben What power?

Fritz The power to control our lives ...

Ben Ah — now you're asking ...

Fifi Perhaps it's because they walk on their hind legs ...

Ben Could be — could be ...

Fritz No — I don't think so ...

Fifi What then?

Fritz (*wisely*) It could be something they call God.

Ben You do know a lot, Fritz ...

Fritz I had a human once ... Oh, he was a strange one — he talked of this God all the time: "God knows," he would say, "God knows."

Ginger He might know where my brothers and sisters are.

Fifi This God — is he the one they talk to every time a bell rings? They pick something up in their paw and say "Hallo?" Is that God, do you suppose?

Fritz No. I know about this. No, this is not God. The thing they pick up is called a telephone. Yes. Definitely. A telephone.

Ben A telephone, eh? I've never heard of no telephone.

Fifi But all human homes have them.

Ben Ah — but you see — I've never been in a human home ...

Fritz You must have!

Ben I haven't.

Fifi What about your humans? Where did they live?

Ben I only ever had the one human. And we walked. That's what we did. We walked.

Fifi You mean "Walkies".

Ben (*puzzled*)"Walkies"?

Fifi "Walkies"! They get your lead, put it on your collar, and take you "Walkies". To make "pee pee".

Ginger What's "pee pee"? Is it food? Is it? Is it?

Fifi *(coyly)* Of course not. "Pee pee" is when you ... When you ... *(She is overcome with modesty)*

Fritz Here! I show you. *(He goes to the back of the cage and lifts a leg)* "Pee pee!"

Fifi Disgusting.

Ben Now why go and do one in your cage?

Fritz Huh! I do them where I want to do them.

Fifi *(with a shudder)* Oh ...

Ginger How many humans have you had, Fritz?

Fritz Seven. Or is it eight ... *(He tries to remember; he is deep in thought during the following)*

Fifi I have had three lots of humans. First, I had Mumsie and Popsie. Then when Popsie went away and Mumsie couldn't manage my walkies any more I went to Master and Missus — smaller garden but very nice — and then Master went away and Missus went to live with her daughter. But she had a cat — stupid creature — and it climbed up the curtain every time it saw me so I went to Bobo. She was a friend of Missus. But one day Bobo fell down and didn't get up and a human in a blue coat brought me here.

Ben *(knowledgeably)* Blue coat? That'll be the fuzz ...

Ginger Fuzz? What's fuzz? Is it food? Is it? Is it? *(During the following, he becomes bored with all the talking and falls asleep)*

Fritz Nine. I have had nine humans.

Ben Nine, eh? That's an awful lot.

Fritz Not for an army dog.

Ben Army dog? What's an army dog?

Fritz Oh, army dogs are very special. Highly trained. Disciplined. *(He speaks with great pride)* I — I have guarded perimeters.

They all look at him

Perimeters? Barbed wire? Search lights?

Ben *(none the wiser)* Oh. I still don't see why you've had nine humans ...

Fritz Shall I tell you? Because when these humans have their pups ——

Fifi Humans don't have pups. They have babies. (*To the others*) He knows nothing ...

Fritz Then I hate them, these babies. They cry, they whine, they take food from our bowls. And who gets locked in the shed? Not the babies. Oh no. "Germs," they say. "Think of the germs!"

Ben Sure you don't mean fleas?

Fritz And so one is passed on.

Fifi They are only protecting their young.

Fritz It is us who need protecting. And as for the things they call "toddlers"!

Ben I'm learning something today, I really am. What's a toddler?

Fifi Bigger babies.

Fritz Who stick their fingers in your eyes and pull on your tail and tear out handfuls of your fur and try to ride on your back. And what do the humans do? They laugh! And say "How clever"!

Ginger makes a yelping noise in his sleep. The others look at him

Ben He's a nice little pup ...

Fifi We were all nice little pups ...

Fritz That's true ...

Fifi No-one ever asks us what we want ...

Fritz What would be the point? They think we don't understand.

Ben Ah, now, you're wrong there. My human, he did think I could understand. Used to talk to me all the time, he did.

Fritz Commands. All I ever had were commands. And beatings ...

They sit for a moment thinking of their past lives

Fifi (*dreamily*) I fell in love with a greyhound once ...

The others look at her

Fritz What's that got to do with anything?

Fifi Nothing ...

Fritz (*despairingly*) Silly bitch ...

They sit in silence for a moment

Ben These "germs" — what are they?
Fritz Mm ... I am not absolutely sure but I think they use them when they fight.
Ben Really?
Fritz I think they throw them at each other.
Ben Well, I never. Throw them, eh? And then what?
Fritz Then I think they die.
Ben Die? How big are they then?
Fritz Oh ... small. But — from what I have heard — very powerful.
Ben They want to be careful. I mean what if they all start throwing these germs? And they kill each other off? What then?
Fritz Ah ... That would be the end of the world ...
Ben (*shocked*) And they know that? And they still throw 'em? Humans ...

There is the noise of dogs barking

Fifi (*sniffing the air*) Someone's coming! (*She sniffs again*) Brown Coat and a strange human. It's the visitor.
Ben Is it? (*He sniffs*) I can't scent like what I used to ...
Fritz (*sniffing*) She's right.
Ben Best get ready then. Ginger! Wake up, Ginger!
Ginger What? What? Is it food? Is it? Is it?
Fritz I almost hope they do choose the pup ... "Is it? Is it?" He is driving me mad ...
Ben Look, if one of you lot does get picked — all the best.
Ginger (*wild with excitement*) Me! Me! Me!

The Warden enters L with a Woman

Ginger rushes round in mad circles. Fritz and Fifi shout loudly. The Woman covers her ears against the noise. The Warden tries to calm the dogs

Fifi I will be good. I love babies. I do not bite.
Fritz I am highly trained. I will guard and protect.
Ginger Me! Me! Pick me!
Warden Quiet! Will you be quiet!

The dogs quieten down

That's better. (*To the Woman*) They can't help it. They're excited.
Woman Bless them ...
Warden It's not the usual visiting time, you see. They don't know what's going on.
Fritz Oh please ...
Woman It's so good of you to let me come round late.
Warden Not at all. If it gets one of them a home I'll show you round at midnight.
Fritz Midnight! Never mind us ...

The warden moves to Ginger's cage; the Woman follows

Fifi Nice scent ...
Ginger Me! Me! Pick me!
Woman (*at Ginger's cage*) Isn't he sweet?
Ben Play your cards right, Ginge.
Ginger What's cards? Is it food? Is it? Is it?
Warden This is Ginger. Should be in the puppy block, really, but we're full to bursting in there. Nice little dog. Excitable. But easily trained.
Ginger Yes! Yes! (*He holds up a paw*)
Fritz Exhibitionist.
Woman Ah ... I wish I could take them all ...
Ben I'd like a bone for every time I've heard that.
Woman But I don't think I could take on a puppy. Not with the children.
Fritz Uh-huh! She has young.
Fifi I don't care. I'm good with human young. They can ride on my back.
Fritz Don't cheapen yourself.

Warden Quiet! (*Hoping to sell her Ginger*) Nice for kids to grow up with a dog.

Woman I know, but my sister's got a puppy. And when she brings it over it's absolute chaos. Tears round and round. Chews everything in sight.

Fifi What did I tell you ...

Warden It's only a phase ...

Woman Not one I can cope with, I'm afraid.

Warden How many children have you got?

Woman Four.

Fritz I would drown the lot.

Woman Two at school and two still at home.

Warden You've got your hands full.

Woman And actually ... (*she laughs*)

Warden Not another one?

Woman Gluttons for punishment, aren't we?

Ben
Fritz } (*together*) Yes.
Fifi

Woman Sorry little puppy — but I hope someone takes you and loves you.

Ginger turns away and slumps

Woman They're almost human, aren't they?

Fritz Please don't insult us.

The Woman moves to Ben

Warden That's old Ben. Beautiful nature. Gentle as a lamb.

Woman What's his history?

Warden Sad story, belonged to some dirty old tramp. Inseparable, they were. Must have always been together. And when the old boy died they found Ben sitting by the body. Had a hell of a job to get him away.

Ben is shocked by what he has heard

Woman Oh, doesn't it break your heart? How old is he then?

Warden Well, as far as the vet can make out nine or ten. Good age. And considering he's always been on the road he's in fair shape. Lovely natured dog.

Woman Mm ... (*She moves on to Fritz*) German Shepherd?

Warden Yes. Well, cross breed.

Fifi Ha!

Woman What are they like with kiddies?

Fritz Throw me one and I will show you.

Warden Fine. He's been with a lot of children, never been any trouble.

Woman Really?

Ben You're in with a chance.

Fritz We will see about that! (*He moves close to the Woman and lifts his leg*)

The Woman steps back, horrified

Warden Fritz! That's not like him, normally they all do that outside.

Woman Is he house trained?

Warden They said he was ...

Woman (*pointing to the back of the cage*) He's done one there.

Warden Maybe he's got a bit of a chill ...

Woman Oh, I don't want to take him on if he's delicate.

Fritz coughs

Oh, no. I don't think so. (*She moves to Fifi*)

The Warden follows the Woman, giving Fritz a worried look

Is this a poodle?

Fritz shakes with laughter

Fifi I have won prizes!

Warden Our Fifi. Yes, she needs a good trim, of course ——
Fifi Yes, yes!
Warden — and she's very overweight at the moment ——
Fifi Walkies! I have had no walkies for months.
Warden Trouble is she's always been with old people who've given her titbits from morning till night.
Fifi (*longingly*) Titbits ...
Warden But a strict diet and plenty of exercise she'd be a different dog.
Woman The thing is, with kiddies, they will give them food all the time. We're on our fourth lot of goldfish. They keep killing them with kindness. And I'm not sure about the exercise.
Warden All dogs need exercise.
Woman Oh, I know. But I couldn't take on a dog that needed ten miles a day. (*She looks along the cages*)
Warden (*indicating the dogs*) Well, this is it ...
Fritz This human is wasting our time.
Woman That's the lot, isn't it?
Warden I'm afraid it is. But don't worry, we have new ones coming in all the time.

The Woman goes back to Ben

Woman There's something about this one — Ben, did you say?
Warden Ben, yes. Look, what exactly are you looking for?
Woman I suppose I want a dog for me, really. My husband's always busy; he's a builder, out all hours, I'm always doing things for the children, I want — someone for me. (*She looks at Ben*) What sort of an age do you think he'll get to?
Warden Well, with a good home ——
Woman He'd have that.
Warden — lots of care, lots of love, could go on for another five or six years.
Woman Beautiful eyes ...
Warden Be lovely if you did take him. I don't want to twist your arm at all but he's already been here much longer than he should. And if he doesn't go by Friday — and I never thought he would

— I'm afraid he's going to be put to sleep. We don't like doing it but with so many dogs coming in all the time sometimes we just have to.

Fritz and Fifi look at Ben with deep sympathy. Ben is seemingly unaware and deep in thought

Let me get him out, see what you think. (*He opens the cage*) Come on, old fella, come and make friends.

After some thought Ben comes slowly to the front of the cage. The Woman approaches him. She kneels and scratches his ears

Woman Hallo? You're a nice old boy, aren't you? You like that, don't you? That's nice, isn't it?
Warden Why not have a think about it? Give us a ring tomorrow?
Woman No, he's the one for me.

The Woman scratches Ben's ears, smiling. Suddenly Ben snarls and snaps at her hand. She screams. Ben retreats

Warden (*slamming the door shut*)You bad, bad dog!

Ben cowers

(*To the Woman*) I'm so sorry ...
Woman (*very shaken*) It's all right — it's just a graze.
Warden I can't understand it. He's always been so gentle ——
Woman He seemed so sweet-natured. Maybe he was frightened.
Warden Whatever the reason we can't have that. He'll be put down first thing in the morning. Can't risk waiting till Friday. It might happen again.
Woman (*obviously shocked*) If he'd done that to one of the children ...
Warden (*looking at the Woman's hand*) We'd better put some disinfectant on that. Come and have a cup of tea.

The Warden moves the Woman away, stopping to shout at Ben

You bad, bad dog.

Ben cowers in a corner

The Warden and the Woman exit

Ginger What's happening? Is it, Ben? Is it? Is it?

Fritz and Fifi ignore Ginger and look at Ben

Fritz Why? Why?
Fifi She was a nice human. She would have been good to you. You would have had a wonderful life. Walkies. Titbits. Love — you would have been loved.
Ben I've been loved.
Fritz You heard what he said? You were going to White Coat on Friday.
Ben Well, now I'm going tomorrow.
Fritz It was me. Telling you about the toddlers. They are not so bad. Once you get used to them ...
Ben No, Fritz, no — it wasn't that. It was him. Brown Coat. Talking about my human ... What did he call him — "dirty old tramp"? My human was the best, the very best ... Know where he found me? Hanging up. Rope round me neck and a crowd throwing stones at me. Took the lot on, he did. He threw 'em this way and that. Then he got me down, put me in his coat, and knocked on a door and asked for milk. "I've never begged before," he said "but this pup needs milk." Wanted to take me in, they did. Said I'd have a good home. But he wouldn't part with me. "He'll do all right with me," he said. "We'll get on." And we did. We slept in ditches, we slept in fields, some nights we were that cold ... But we'd snuggle up together — we were fine. The two of us. Fine. And we walked. Rain, shine, didn't matter. And we talked. All the time. I knew he was getting tired. Some days we didn't get on the road till ... Well, some days we didn't get on the road at all. He'd just lay there. "We'll eat tomorrow, Ben," he'd say — 'cos we shared everything. Then this one day — he didn't wake up. "He's tired," I thought,

"walked too far." So I got up close to him, to keep him warm, like, and just — stayed. Waiting for him to wake up ... Then they came. I kept telling them he was only asleep but all they did was put a muzzle on me ...

Fritz Was he cold?

Ben Stone cold... (*He is motionless during the following*)

Fritz Then he was dead.

Fifi Don't!

Fritz It's better he knows.

Ginger What's dead?

Fritz Dead is the end. When there is nothing more. Your eyes close and never open.

Ginger Like sleeping?

Fifi Yes. yes, like sleeping.

Ben I wondered why he never came for me. 'Cos I knew he would. When he woke up ... All this time I've been waiting for him.

Fifi Oh, Ben! Ben! The thought of you — not being here. I can't bear it ...

Ben Now then, Fifi, now then. I had the choice.

Ginger Is Ben going? Is he? Is he?

Fritz Yes. He is. And he is a fool. (*To Ben*) I have some biscuit. You can have it all.

Ben Ta, Fritz. I'll — maybe eat it later. Just at the minute I'm not feeling — quite the ticket. (*He crouches down*) I shouldn't have done that. That was wrong of me. Never done it before. But — I couldn't have gone with her. Not after the life I had with — with him.

Fifi Oh ... I want to go to him ... He should not be in there alone.

Fritz You can't. We are caged.

Ben It's gone very cold, hasn't it? Very cold ...

Fifi looks at Fritz. She makes to speak. Fritz shakes his head at her

Fritz Yes, it has. Very cold.

Ben I can't ever remember — feeling — so cold ... (*He shivers, stretches out, shivers again, then is still*)

Fifi Oh ...

Ginger Ben? Ben? (*He goes to the bars, sniffs, shivers, then backs away*)

Fifi No White Coat ... I am so glad ...

Fritz Yes .... Good to know they do not have complete power ...

All three dogs sit in silence

Then we hear the sound of barking from all the dogs in the kennels; the sound rises in a crescendo

The Lights fade to Black-out

FURNITURE AND PROPERTY LIST

On stage: Four blanket beds. *Under* **Ginger**'s: biscuit
          A few rubber toys for **Ginger** to chew

Personal: **Warden**: chocolate buttons , notebook, pen

LIGHTING PLOT

Practical fittings required: nil
Interior. The same throughout

To open: General interior lighting

Cue 1   Sound of dogs barking rises to a crescendo   (Page 19)
          Fade lights to black

EFFECTS PLOT

Cue 1   When ready   (Page 1)
         Sudden noise of loud barking

Cue 2   **Fritz**: "Ah — they are telling him ..."   (Page 1)
         Slowly fade barking to silence

Cue 3   **Ben**: "Humans ..."   (Page 11)
         Noise of dogs barking

Cue 4   **Fritz**: " ... complete power ...". Silence   (Page 19)
         Sound of barking from many dogs;
         rise to crescendo

Lightning Source UK Ltd.
Milton Keynes UK
UKHW020954110422
401398UK00006B/476

9 780573 121753